## Also by Alexis Rhone Fancher

*How I Lost My Virginity to Michael Cohen &*
     *other heart stab poems* (Sybaritic Press, 2014)

*State of Grace: The Joshua Elegies* (KYSO Flash Press, 2015)

*Enter Here* (KYSO Flash Press, 2017)

*Junkie Wife* (Moon Tide Press, 2018)

*The Dead Kid Poems* (KYSO Flash Press, 2019)

# EROTIC

## New & Selected

Alexis Rhone Fancher

**Books**™

The New York Quarterly Foundation, Inc.
Beacon, New York

NYQ Books™ is an imprint of The New York Quarterly Foundation, Inc.

The New York Quarterly Foundation, Inc.
P. O. Box 470
Beacon, NY 12508

www.nyq.org

First Edition

Set in New Baskerville

Layout by Raymond P. Hammond

Cover Layout by James A. Fancher and Alexis Rhone Fancher

Cover Photo: "Self-Portrait" by Alexis Rhone Fancher 2019

Cover Font: Subway Novella, Licensed by KC Fonts

Library of Congress Control Number: 2020949308

ISBN: 978-1-63045-071-7

# EROTIC

## New & Selected

*For Kate O'Donnell*
*(1949–2014)*

# Contents

# EROTIC

## New & Selected

*"Bumpy Night"* 2018

# Handy

I wanted you small and folded
in my pocket. Like a Swiss Army knife.
Like a blow up doll. I wanted you
to fuck me and then disappear.
You wanted me wide open,
surrendered. Like a vacation.
Like a ripe nectarine.
I wanted to use you for sex.
Isn't that what all
men dream of?
You wanted to fuse us
to the bed, glue me, on my hands
and knees, to the sheet, through
the mattress, tether me to the box
springs, nail me through
the floor.
That day I saw you in Venice,
you walked past me
like your cock had
never been in my mouth.
I almost grabbed a fistful of you,
crammed you in like food.

## Tonight I Will Dream of Anjelica, My First Ex-Girlfriend, Who Taught Me the Rules of the Road...

Anjelica comes on to me like a man, all slim-hipped swagger, relentless, dangling that red, '57 T'Bird at me like dessert. Lemme take you for a ride, chica, she sez after acting class. I figure what's the harm, but Ms Angel Food gets out of hand. I don't count on her heart-shaped ass, or those brown nipples crammed in my mouth. I don't count on the Dial-O-Matic four-way, power leather seats, the telescoping steering wheel, or the frantic pleasure of her face between my thighs. I admit, I've always been driven to sin. But Anjelica's far from blameless. She rides me hard, week after week, double clutches me into ecstasy, hipbone against hipbone, the dulcet, lingering groan of our gears, grinding. When I confess the affair to my boyfriend he jacks himself off in the galley kitchen, comes all over his unattainable fantasies. He says he doesn't consider sex between women to be cheating, and begs me to set up a threesome. I tell him the T'Bird's a two-seater, and watch his face fall. I could end it, but why? All I can say is, I want her for myself. All I can say is, I'm a die-hard romantic. Anyone I do, I do for love.

# poem for my new boyfriend with oversized blue lips tattooed on his neck

Is it your ex's pout? I wonder. Blue
and on your neck. Full lips, parted
like an invitation—

a visual love poem.

Daytime, I keep to your good side,
your skin unsullied.

But in the night while you sleep
I match my lips to the imprint

tongue the moue
of my predecessor's mouth,
lick her salty legacy,
and come up thin.

I can't sleep for wondering
if she's for real,

if she wore your pants,
mouthed your prayers,
sucked you off like a Hoover?

I want them to be some stranger's lips.
Clip art, a souvenir of a 3-day bender
in the company of sailors.

Instead, after whisky and kinky sex,
one night you let it slip:

how just before she kissed you off
she led you on a leash,
sat you in the chair,
cupped your chin,

imprinted her lipsticked kiss
on your neck's throbbing pulse,

and ordered the tattooist to begin.

# Tonight We Will Bloom for One Night Only

Tonight you must plow me a respite between the moonflowers,
mock orange, night phlox, and Epiphyllum Oxypetalum.
You must open me to the summer night like cereus.

You must pick my perversions like petals, allow them
for one night to bloom, frangipani wafting, a concupiscent
wind humming at my door.

I've surrendered to your heady sweat of primrose, plumeria,
addicted to your outstretched arms of night-blooming jasmine,
my heliotrope buds hard and wanting, reeking of Madagascar vanilla
with its accompanying moral ambiguity.

I am more than a day lily.

We are each bodies, hard-wired for pleasure,
destined for momentary blooming,
then extinction.

When the bats swarm and the moths sidle up to this one night
of fevered pollination, let's be ready.

Let's face them, our appetency the headlights
    they slam into again and again.

We will make our escape at first light. Singing.

# Mixed Signals

Look, I know lust when I see it.

Those nipples poke through her T-shirt
like it's my birthday.

Tonight, I'm ripe for forgiveness.
Tonight, she's hardwired for love.

So when she asks me to sleep in the spare room,
makes up the futon, brings me a pillow from her bed,

I'm on high alert.

She knows that pillow exudes her perfume,
but she gives me the cold shoulder,

rebuffs the kisses she once savored,
when she licked her lips for the taste of me.

*Don't*, she warns.

Her mouth says one thing—her body another.
Now she's a waiting conversation; I'm the lame excuse.

If I were a man she'd tell me to keep it in my pants.
If I were a man, perhaps she'd treat me better.

Tonight, dozing at her feet,
I fall again for her painted toes—

her impossibly high expectations,
the crushing payback of her heel.

## this small rain

this small rain sambas on San Vicente
wanders through Whittier
mambos past Montebello
and East LA

this small rain moves like a Latina
over-plucks her eyebrows
drinks Tequila shooters
fronts a girl-band

this small rain works two jobs
dawdles in downpours
this small rain seeds clouds

this small rain drives to Vegas in a *tormenta*
has a friend in Jesus
needs boots and a winter coat

in this drought-wracked city,
this small rain dreams of flash floods,
*depósitos*, indigo lakes,
cisterns, high water,
Big Gulps, endless refills

in this drought-wracked city,
this small rain settles on the *hierba seca*
sleeps under freeways
plays the lotto
is unlucky in love

this small rain longs to hose down the highways
this small rain chases storms

this small rain has a tsunami in her heart

this small rain kamikaze's
in the gutter
suicides on summer sidewalks
dreams of a deluge
that overflows the river banks
washes L.A. clean

in this drought-wracked city,
this small rain scans the heavens,
looking for a monsoon,
searching for *su salvador*
in the reclaimed desert sky.

*"Clubbing, Midnight: 6th & Spring, DTLA"* 2016

# Cousin Elaine from Chicago and I Are Naked

In the space between taking off our clothes
and putting on our swimsuits,

we stand naked.
My chest is flat as a board.

Her curves are already legendary,
her breasts bursting from her bikini.

I want to run my fingers along
their goosebumped perimeter,
lick their chocolate tips.

I am 12 and shouldn't think this way.

I shouldn't think about her tanned legs
thrown over mine on the couch,
nights when we watch TV, shouldn't

think about the damp between my thighs
when she bunks with me at night,

when dreams of following her back to Chicago
consume my sleep.

In the pool, she's a silver fish;
my body's a heat-seeking missile.

"Marco!" she calls from the deep end,
her eyes shut tight.

"Polo!" I whisper in her shell ear.
When I reach for her she does not pull away.

When she kisses me, open-mouthed, I pull
the string on her bikini, free her breasts,
bury my lips between them.

When I speak of this day in our far off future,
she'll say it never happened, swear it was all a dream.

# Like Sisyphus at the Chateau Marmont

I'd slip out of my skirt, my thong,
*(my attitude),*

pull the sweater
over my head.

Arrange my body
on the bed.

I'd go wet at the thought of you.
It washed me clean
and stupid.

Down on all fours like a fucking dog,
doing what my mama warned me
not to do, throwing good
money after bad.

Did I mention how much I liked it?

We had a history,
all dead ends.

You brought the handcuffs
I'd make amends.

We already know exactly
how it ends.

You lie. I believe.
I submit, you deceive.

My body turns to you like a dahlia
seeks the sun

and then you run.

*"Rainy Night, DTLA" 2016*

# Don't Wash

"I'm returning in three days. Don't wash."
—From a love letter Napoleon sent to Josephine

I touch myself so I can savvy what you rut in. Bring my fingers to my mouth, imagine you in our bed, returned from the three-day fray, redolent of the weight of the world, and me, your dirty, dirty girl, naked, eager, as you make your way down, breathing in my hair, my lips, the sweet spot where neck meets collarbone. I've made a religion of your fantasies, a science of what you desire. That ferine moan, my always startled gasp at first thrust. I angle, cocked hips, a bit askew. I arch for maximum penetration. Our bed is a rocket launch, a bacchanal, a pelican's steep dive into the sea. For Michael, my first love, I used the freshening wipe before I arrived, so as not to offend. I spread myself wide on his bed, confident, watching the top of his head (black curls) as he explored me — that fear of not being Summer's Eve™ fresh, worried my pussy might disenchant, the musk of me—all wiped away. He raised his head. *Next time,* Michael said, *don't wash.*

# L'appel du vide

The romance is gone. I forget to bathe. Soon I'll have eaten all the mangoes.
*Try to think,* my lover says, foot out the door, *of the big picture.*

Today when I heard the garage door open my heart jumped and I thought
of it, the "big picture." *I want you not to have fucked her in our bed,*"I want to say.

*It's not all bad,* he answers. *We have similar taste in women.* This is not the first time
he's waved romance in my face.

*This pandemic,* he says. *It's breakin' my balls.* His big hands cup my ass.

At midnight, I drive downtown. A straight shot on the 110 N, but for the over/
underpass near Watts where I want to swerve into oncoming traffic but,
of course, there is none.

I return to remnants of moonlight and shut the blinds, but the truth persists,
insidious; a germ. The mango bowl: a hole now, nothing but air.
And his voice diddling the dark.

## This Is NOT a Poem

This is NOT a poem. Bam! This is an assault to your senses, a rape of your status quo. This is NOT a poem, not some trendy leopard print, not a polka dot parade. No. You do not smell hot dogs, cotton candy or frankincense. The myrrh has left the building. This is NOT a poem. It's an anthem, a declaration of noncompliance, a liberation proclamation. Snap! Snap! This is NOT a poem. It's a love song, a torch song, a song of myself and NOT you. No tears, got it? Don't act like a girl. Blow your nose wipe your eyes. Don't make yourself look stupid! This is NOT a poem. It's salt poured on the wound. Can it feel? Only if I let it burn too deeply. This is NOT a poem. No! It isn't good enough. No. I've read poems & it's not the same. Snap! Snap! This is NOT a poem. It's a hip hop of my own creation, a celebration of my brains my breasts my underground caverns. This is NOT a poem. It's a rite of passage, a starry night, a reluctant homage to your name, spelled out in lonely Broadway lights. My life goes dark without you, honey. Clap! Clap! This is NOT a poem. You with your lust, with your X-ray eyes. Listen up now. Be careful how you love me. Be grateful for second chances. Don't push too hard. I might surprise you. You'll see, I'm tougher than I look: I eat Bukowski for breakfast.

# I Want Louboutin Heels

I want Louboutin heels,
with those trademark red soles,
I want them sexy, I want them high,
I want them slingback and peep-toed
so I can flash the purple polish
on my tootsies.

I want to wear them out of the store,
just you try and stop me.

I want to wow them
on Washington, saunter past C&O Trattoria
and Nick's Liquor Mart, those bottles of Stoli
stacked in the window, calling my name,

past the summer-clad tourists in December,
shivering, barefoot, like LA has no winter.

In those shoes I'm hot,
stop-a-truck hot,
prettiest girl in school hot,
and this time, I know it.
Flaunt it. Hell, I own it. In those shoes
I can pick and choose, not settle for some loser.

Not drink away regrets, pound back Stoli
at Chez Jay's, flash their scarlet bottoms
when I kneel.

I'll wear them like my own flesh,
like hooves, like sin.
I'll keep their secrets, won't spill
where they've been.

Better those shoes with their lurid soles
than you with yours.

*(For Laurie Quinn Seiden)*

29

## I Was Hovering Just below the Hospital Ceiling, Contemplating My Death

When I glanced down and saw my body,
the suffering, damaged girl.

My beloved, nowhere to be found
had died on impact.

Now the ER doctors say I can go either way.

So I hover on the Sistine ceiling
of the I.C.U., undecided, my dead lover's
hand reaching for me
like God stretched for Adam.

The tubes and machines that keep me
earthbound give way.

We soar above the hospital morgue,
backtrack the highway, our bodies
unbroken, the crash spliced out.

My mother keens beside my hospital bed,
her fingers tangled in my blood-soaked hair,
picking at pieces of windshield.
Holding tight.

Years later I re-trace the road
between death and Santa Barbara,
how he cradled my head in his lap as he drove.

How he didn't want to go with me.
How I always got what I wanted.

All my life, such a greedy girl.

*(When I was twenty, a highway collision killed my fiancé and my unborn child. I survived only because I was asleep, my head on my fiancé's lap, when the driver of the other vehicle veered into our lane and crashed into us at 70mph. I have tried for years to write about the immediate aftermath. This poem is the first time I got it right.)*

30

*"Club Kids, 6th & Spring, DTLA"* 2016

# Lunatic Poem #1

*"Would you be a moon for the lunatics here?"\**

I'm already looney. Pick me.

The *luna plena* sneaks in from the high window.

You burrow between
my legs, howl and howl.

Some people can turn into wolves just
by wanting to become one.

I bet this happens all the time.

You're Nicholson and then
you're the wolf.

No one ever mentions the bite—
the ecstasy of the wounding.

At no time do I stare you in the eyes.

I bare my throat to you.
Then I disappear.


*(\* a line from "After The Tour, or A Tirade on Shitville," a poem by Michael Farrell.)*

# Lunatic Poem #2

## The Downside of Love

I've had better-looking suitors. Better mannered. Better dressed. They know to wipe their feet at the door, to rise when a lady leaves the room. Punctuality is always a sore spot between us. Easily distracted, he can smell pussy a mile away. I've been treated better, too. Been taken out for dinner instead of having it dropped at my feet. Even that might be okay, but it's rarely just the two of us. The thing about wolves? They run in a pack. And if I manage to pull him away, those yellowed fangs! That gamey breath! Try, just try to get him to the dentist. Truth told, his hair's too wiry, his nostrils perpetually flared. When I reach for him at night, his nose is cold. He's too hot to sleep with in the summer. In winter, he's lumbering and slow to rouse. But ah! The snuggled heat of his belly when the snow falls, the nuzzle of his muzzle against my clit, the moon-shattering scream when I come.

## Let's Be Happy Now!

Danny looks at me, the way
they all do:
lust-eyes. He waylays me
in the bathroom, hairy arms suddenly
around my waist.
"I heard U fucking Mickey last night,"
he says, "heard U cry out,
& no, no
it wasn't a cat but it yowled,
U yowled and my dick got hard, baby.
U know U want it. Deny it & I'll call U
a fucking liar.
I don't care who we hurt!
Let's be happy now!"

I confess,
his recklessness holds a certain allure,
& then I'm fuckin' him real high
& hard, up against the sink
in the bathroom, with his soon-to-be
wife just outside,
ear pressed against the door.
Not the marrying kind.
I'm the fucking kind.
The lewd lingerie kind.
The girl you
bring home for
the weekend,
not to meet the family
kind.
The dirty little secret,
the girl you jack off to after
your wife
goes to sleep.
The one you think about
so you can get it up with
the old lady,

year after year,
decade after dreary
decade. The one you wish you'd married
& you'd be happy now,
happy now,
so very happy,
now.

# Sex, Guns, and the Canadians Next Door...

*After Edward Hopper's painting, "Eleven AM 1926"*

*A big caliber bullet goes in like a dime and comes out like a cash register,*
M says. His gun is out of the case. He fancies himself a thrill killer.
Or a poet. It's August. Muggy. The air in the apartment so thick,
M's innuendo can't reach me. Across the alley, the Canadian couple
are at it again; wild fucking with the drapes wide and lights on, a
tutorial for we less fortunates. He's a big man, hulking, and she,
sweet blonde with multiple piercings, straddles him like a horse.
They're smooth-skinned. Athletic. These days, all I do is watch. Me
and M, we don't fuck like that anymore; a girl slips up just *one* time,
and the permanent cold shoulder. Like he was such an angel? *That's
different,* he says. *Sorry,* I don't say again. Instead, I stare across the
alley into my neighbors' lives. I'm naked, the way M likes me, (but
for those black kitten heels he insists I wear), and I play with myself
while he plays with his gun, just out of frame. I'm hoping he'll get
the message, that I'm horny enough to make it up to him and try
again, or just rut, no strings. But he's consumed with a different kind
of gun, his big-bulleted, Smith & Wesson 38. Massages it with linseed
oil, ramrods the barrel.

*"110 Freeway South, DTLA"* 2017

# Nebraska

"We never talk," he said, gathering his clothes off the floor. "If my dick got soft, you wouldn't even know me." His defection took me by surprise. "I feel like a stud horse," he muttered. Like that was a bad thing. That last night we lay spooned in what I thought was the afterglow. For the first time since I'd left for college, I felt my life was together. He looked like Robert Redford, his body farmhand hard, already leathered; he smelled like sunlight on the plains. I called him "Nebraska," and when I thought of him, I pictured him with a blade of straw between his teeth the *exact* color of his hair. We'd meet Wednesdays and Saturdays, screw our brains out. Sometimes I'd even cook him dinner.

# Ce Qui Importe (What Matters)

How there can be no daylight between us,
a magnetic field,
a seamless glue.

How desire hardwires my nipples,
how I want you to bring them
to your face.

How you nibble my labia,
and then, there's your tongue—
like an electric grid.

How your fingers zap their way
to my center,
plugged in, like a socket.

How your cock
bends into me,
an over-amping arc.

How I straddle your face,
legs parted so you see no light,
only me, sticky,

and juiced.

# For the Sad Waitress at the Diner in Barstow

beyond the kitchen's swinging door,
beyond the order wheel and the pass-through piled
high with bacon, hash browns, biscuits and gravy,

past the radio, tuned to 101.5-FM
*All Country—All the Time,*
past the truckers overwhelming the counter,
all grab-ass and longing.

in the middle of morning rush
you'll catch her, in a wilted pink uniform,
coffee pot fused in her grip, staring over
the top of your head.

you'll follow her gaze, out the fly-specked, plate
glass windows, past the parking lot,

watch as she eyes those 16-wheelers barreling
down the highway, their mud guards
adorned with chrome silhouettes of naked women
who look nothing like her.

the cruel sun throws her inertia in her face.
this is what regret looks like.

maybe she's searching for that hot day in August
when she first walked away from you.

there's a choking sound
a semi makes, when it pulls off
the highway; that downshift a death rattle
she's never gotten used to.

maybe she's looking for a way back.
maybe she's ready to come home.

(but for now) she's lost herself
between the register and the door, the endless
business from table to kitchen,

she's as much leftover as those sunny side eggs,
yolks hardening on your plate.

*"Waitresses, Redwood Bar, DTLA"* 2015

# The First Time I Made Cousin Lisa Come

We'd been playing doctor for months by then,
her huge breasts a magnet, her soft mons

a refuge from my impending adolescence. Some
nights, unable to dream, I'd touch myself like Lisa,

replay the us, hidden between twin beds in her pink,
frou frou bedroom, my aunt across the hall, making dinner,

the door half open, my fingers three thick in her daughter's
pussy, the pin point of Lisa's nipple stuffed in my mouth.

I'd suck. She'd moan. I'd explore. She'd explode.
It was the most powerful I'd ever be.

The first time I made cousin Lisa come
we looked into each other's aloneness; the boys

who didn't want us yet, the girls who shunned us
like they saw something we didn't.

When I let myself remember:
me, on my knees, between the beds,

the feast of Lisa spread before me,
her steady rocking against my wrist

the rug burn that my knees endured
a penance, prepaid.

# Poem for What's Missing

After she killed herself she went looking
for her lover,
who was three years dead.

She wanted to tell him how it was
no use.

How she'd tried counseling, meditation
and Ambien,
tried losing herself in commercial real estate
and knitting.

She'd adopted yet another cat.
Resumed drinking, stopped
going to the gym.

She'd focused on their steamy nights
spent kissing and kissing,
but she could no longer bring herself
to orgasm.

On his deathbed he promised
they'd reunite.

She dragged herself from the sofa
to their bed, traversed a despair
of *Law & Order* reruns
and vodka.

He'd made her
forget her loveless childhood,
and her two bad marriages.

He'd made her
believe she could finally be
loved.

Anyone who knew her should have seen it coming.
The gym was her religion.

The friends who discovered her body found the cats,
keening.

*I was starved to death,* she told her lover
when she found him.

She wanted to swallow him whole.


*(For Laurie Quinn Seiden and Gary Seiden)*

# How I Lost My Virginity to Michael Cohen

1.  My daddy hated him.
2.  So his best friend, J.R., picked me up. Shook my daddy's hand at the doo
    Promised me back by midnight.
3.  Daddy thought I was obedient, a good girl.
4.  It was hot, even for August.
5.  J.R.'s parents were in Vegas, so he loaned us their bedroom.
    5a.) They had a king-sized bed.
6.  Diana Ross and the Supremes were singing "Baby Love."
7.  J.R. watched cartoons in the den.
8.  Michael's middle finger furrowed between my thighs.
9.  I felt that familiar wetness.
10. Except it wasn't my finger.
11. I remembered where I was and closed my eyes.
12. He pulled down my panties.
13. Pushed up my skirt.
14. No one had put their lips down there before.
15. No one.
16. It felt delicious.
17. I hoped he liked my scent.
18. There were lilies on the nightstand.
19. "Your hair smells so good," he mumbled.
20. He was holding his cock while he licked me.
21. I had never come before.
    21a.) Not like that.
22. It was then I knew I loved him.
23. He tasted like me.
24. His dick grew too big for my mouth.
25. When he entered me, it didn't hurt.
26. "I thought you were a virgin," he said.
27. I thought of the dildo that pleasured me in secret.
28. "Horseback riding," I said.
29. When the rubber broke, he promised he wouldn't come inside me.
30. He promised.

# I'd Never Slept with a Mexican before, He Would Only Do It in the Dark

ON THE ROAD

I had a knife with me that day,
I don't know why.

We just started driving upstate.
When I asked where we were going
he said, "Coffee."

He was too short for me anyway.

*In my dream there was poison in the coffee.*
*It tasted sweet. I didn't seem to mind.*

IN THE DINER

There were miles between us,
a Mojave.

"It's okay to smoke," he said.
"As long as you're not a train."

When he reached for my hands
I saw tattooed saints on his wrists
where the long sleeves shortened.

He let go like he'd been burned.

Folded. A barricade. A moat.

I fondled the knife in my purse
till he caught my eye.

"Keep 'em where I can see 'em."

I could live with that.

*"Mary Fae Smith, Venice Beach"* 2012

## IN THE MOTEL

We danced in the open space
between the queen bed and the door.
He sweated through his button down,
a silver crucifix at his throat,
looked like Marc Anthony
in the motel marquee's light.

Free Cable. Free Ice. No Vacancy.

He kicked off his pants, turned out the light.
Fucked me with his shirt on.

## IN THE MORNING

I surprised him in the shower,
saw his tattooed glory, sleeves,
the American eagle
full-winged across his chest,
"Semper Fi" emblazoned on
a ribbon in its mouth.

I threw the knife out the window
once the car passed Santa Barbara.

"The road is the journey," he said,
the sin of regret in his eyes.

# We carry our identity on our fingertips

When you think that I'm not looking,
you bring your fingers to your nose.
*We carry our identity on our fingertips,*

you say, *pattern recognition-based,*
*all those whorls and arches.*
I'd know them anywhere, baby,

your ridges, and loops,
how fiercely they grip and throttle.
Tonight I slice the garlic, season the roast,

rub cinnamon, brown sugar, pepper
and salt into the meat.
Sear it evenly on all eight sides.

When I bring my fingers to my nostrils, I smell dinner;
when I bring them to yours, you smell love.
I watch you scrape those tasty bits

from the bottom of the pot,
deglaze with beef broth and merlot.
We tie the rosemary sprigs with twine;

float them above the nascent gravy,
chopped onions the crown on top.
You set the timer for 70 minutes,

program the Instant Pot for quick release.
Meanwhile, in the bedroom, we've got time.
You school me in the efficacy

of facial recognition, palm prints, iris I.D.
rub your body all over mine, finger my flesh,
program me for quick release.

# Post Mortem

It's the last time, I swear, except this time I mean it. The last time I mourn Kate so hard I don't eat, unless you consider alcohol a meal. The last time I drive drunk the five miles to Chuck's house, at midnight, despondent, disheveled, swigging Stoli, again, pounding on the door until he lets me in. *I'm not here for small talk,* I tell him. *I'm here to dance away the blues.* I kick off my shoes, unbutton my blouse, but Chuck's uncertain. *You don't have to trust me,* I say, passing him the bottle. When he's drunk enough, I turn off the TV, tell Chuck to *put on something slow.* I want him to remember he loved me once. He puts James Brown on the stereo. *Please Please Me.* Chuck grinds himself against me, like we're still a couple. He pleased me, alright, made me real happy for a month or two; I made him a cliché; fucked his best friend in his galley kitchen. And still, he let me stay.

Tonight we're both shit-faced, slow. Chuck lights a joint. Shows me a photo of Mai Ling, his latest, now that Kate's moved to Santa Fe, abandoned us both. He'd asked her to marry him the week before she left. Stupid fuck. One last time, I want to wallow in our shared loss, tell each other Kate stories till dawn, finally admit that attempted seduction at La Fonda Hotel in Puerto Nuevo, me feeding Kate lobster dipped in melted butter, while she called Chuck each night, feeding him lies. But Chuck's moved on. He's full of this new flame he wants me to meet, how she's is *delicate,* with a *troubled past,* raised in China, to be a *concubine.* As usual, I cut to the chase. *Is she better in the sack than Kate?* Chuck shakes his head. A sore spot. He thinks I stole Kate from him.

The clock in Chuck's kitchen says 4 a.m., and my high is wearing thin. I've had it with all the mourning crap. Like Chuck, I want to move on. So when he asks if I still love her, I tell him I never did. And when he says, *Of all the women in L.A., why Kate?* I tell him how I can't help myself. How I found pleasure in his pain. And when I tell him Kate's the only woman in Hollywood I *haven't* slept with, he laughs in my face. *Look,* I tell him, *she blew us both off.* I can tell I've hit a nerve.

# June Fairchild Isn't Dead

she's planning a comeback.
she's snorting Ajax for the camera.
she's landing a role on "I Spy."
she's writing her number on a napkin and
handing it to me at King Eddy's Saloon.

June Fairchild isn't dead
she's just been voted Mardi Gras Girl at Aviation High.
she's acting in a movie with Roger Vadim.
she's gyrating at Gazarri's, doing the Watusi with Sam The Sham.
she's mainlining heroin in a cardboard box.

June Fairchild isn't dead
I saw her tying one on at King Eddy's Saloon.
she's making "Drive, He Said," with Jack Nicholson.
she's selling the Daily News in front of the courthouse.
she's snorting Ajax for the camera.

June Fairchild isn't dead
she's relapsing in front of the Alexandria Hotel.
she's working as a taxi dancer, making $200 a shift.
I saw her vamping with Hefner, frugging on YouTube.
she's naming Danny Hutton's band *3 Dog Night.*

June Fairchild isn't dead
she's living at the Roslyn SRO on Main.
she's giving up her daughter to her ex.
she's snorting Ajax for the camera.
she's planning a comeback, needs new headshots.

June Fairchild isn't dead
she's Up In Smoke, getting clean.
she's sitting by the phone.
she's falling asleep in Laurel Canyon
with a lit cigarette in her hand,
waiting for me to call.

(Former Gazarri's dancer/film star June Fairchild, a self-proclaimed *"angel in a snake pit,"* died of liver cancer on Feb. 17, 2015. She was 68 years old.)

*"Napkin w/ June Fairchild's Phone Number & Autograph"* 2014

# Eat

Your open 'fridge is the floodlight at a Hollywood premiere, a beacon for gourmands, a newlyminted saint. It lights up Sunset Blvd. from Olivera Street to the beach. Your smile is the blancmange of my sugar crave. It bowls me over, makes me gluttonous, ravenous, makes me eat gelato, and pomme frites, lick pasta with prosciutto in red sauce from the hollow of your throat, makes me want to eat pussy, and cheesecake, and macaroons, wash it all down with a robust Amorone, tamp it down with unfiltered, brown, Sherman cigarettes, makes me want to eat my way down your menu. So I went to Whole Foods to get a chicken, cooked it just the way you like it, with mushrooms and onions and truffle oil, stuffed it with wild rice and naked photos of Ursula Andress, served it in the kitchen of my high-rise on Spring Street, watched you eat it, wolf it down, the same way I'd like to eat you.

*(For Jack Grapes)*

# Polaroid SX-70 Land Camera

There's a reckless streak in me I can't control. It makes me do dangerous things. I know it's wrong, but I always fail—no willpower at all. The thing about Wayne, I tried to keep my distance, but he was hot, sexy in a middle-aged sort of way. He reminded me of some of my father's friends. I thought we were kindred spirits.

"I dream about you at night," he said, his voice husky, low. His breath smelled like clove gum and cigarettes. "I dream you do everything I tell you." He stepped into the small office in the back, came back with a Polaroid SX70, smiled and handed me the camera. "I want you to go into my office, pull down your panties, spread your legs and shoot a photo for me. You know what I want. Something really hot."

The phone rang. He picked it up. "Wayne's Volkswagen Repair." He turned back to me, leering. "I'll make it worth your while," he said.

I sat on the cold metal stool at the counter, legs crossed, black skirt riding up my thighs. It was a long way from Shangri La. Fenders and transmissions littered the floor, tools hung on pegs nailed into the walls, and half-rebuilt engines balanced on benches and worktops. Every surface was covered with a layer of greasy dust that mingled with Wayne's ever-present cigarette and made the air heavy and hard to breathe. What was it about these sleazy places? I felt sick. My stomach bottomed out with that familiar, crazy swirling. Sickening, but I still craved it. Bad girl with a bad habit. Very, very bad.

I clutched the camera, watched the dust particles swirl in the light shafts from the open door. I could leave, follow the light right out to Lakewood Blvd. Get away this time, before I got in past my depth. Instead I looked inside to where the light ended, where it spotlighted the Rigid Tool calendar with a naked "Miss July" hanging in the place of honor behind the cash register. Someone had given her a mustache. My head hurt from the loud banging, rhythmic, like a clock striking, going all the time. Wayne's two Mexicans pounded metal out back, competing with 40 mph traffic on the street. The Golden Oldies station blared out the hits.

I couldn't hear myself think except to think that Wayne was waiting for an answer. To think that I should get out now, be that lady my mother raised me to be. Cold hands. Cold heart. My mother. I could never tell her, she'd never understand about this. About why I do this. Over and over! About how crazy I get around the wrong kind of man, a man like Wayne, so crazy when he smoothed his black hair back from his face and wiped the sweat on his greasy jeans. Slumming, that's what she'd call it.

But me, I never listened, I was too busy dreaming about how his blue work shirt was half unbuttoned. I could see the thick hair on his chest and the pocket of his shirt that said "Wayne" in big red letters. Crazy for his smell—his hands—big hands, calloused, black in the creases. I wondered what they'd feel like on my skin. I wondered what he meant by "I'll make it worth your while."

Wayne looked right at me as he hung up the phone. "Well," he said. "What's it gonna be?"

# Second Chances

Remember those days in Chatsworth,
before all the porno stars moved in?
We made our own movies.

You'd grab my hips,
push up my dress, whisper obscenities
into my belly, your hot breath
a short cut to nirvana.

I keep thinking about your tongue,
how it could curl up,
twist from side to side,
make a girl very happy.

The last time we met I wore
that Donna Karan sheath
you bought me, the one
with the slit up the side.

It made me look so hot
you swore you wanted
to marry me.

Instead, we took risks. Shot drugs.
Let ourselves be seduced
by strangers.

I've been trying to get back
to you for years.

I keep thinking about your thumbs,
how they arch backward
in double-jointed ecstasy, perfectly
shaped for my clitoral pleasure.

The dress still fits.
I could wear it when you fuck me.
When we move back to Chatsworth,
we'll pretend we never left.

## Dark Options

When you smile in your sleep I get nervous.
I know what you're capable of.
I've got the souvenirs to prove it, the fractured wrist
that never healed, the flinch when
you reach for my face.
I've learned to do what you tell me.
Make myself small.
Shut the fuck up.

Yesterday at the market I bought star fruit, endive, hollow points
and a pair of balls.

Thought I'd give the salad a little kick.
Sandmen have made themselves at home in your lashes.
Dark blood is matted in your hair.
It's 2 a.m. but I'm awake.
I could have shaved my legs, could have blown you when
you asked, stopped being *(what did you call me?)* a withholding bitch.

I like you best comatose, compromised, your back to me.

Red is your color.

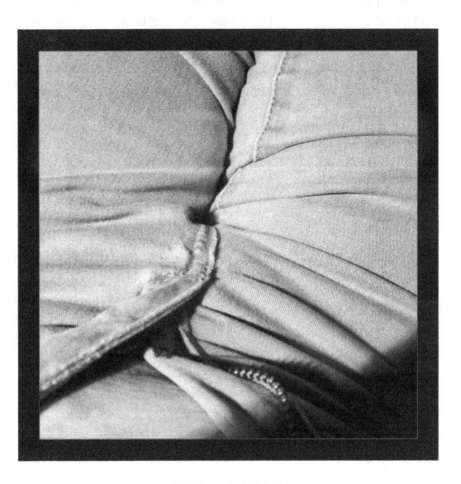

*"Self-Portrait #1" 2011*

# Red-Handed in Canoga Park: Root Causes & How It Is All My Fault

*(A Sister Poem)*

We were five, and three. You sat behind me on my blue bike, hung on tight the four blocks to the drugstore. They had toys. Paddle Ball, Jacks, stuffed animals. I was entranced by the My Merry Kitchen set. Thumb-sized boxes of Ivory Snow, Kleenex, Ajax, and my favorite, a perfect replica bottle of Windex. The stuff of my dollhouse dreams. The restraint I had exhibited on previous visits failed me. I jabbed my finger through the cellophane, that tiny, blue bottle irresistible. You palmed the Clorox, reached for the Brillo pads. "Hey!" the manager shouted, his bigness looming down the aisle. There was no place to hide.When I ran, you froze. When I got on my bike and sped off, you faced the music. This day has defined our sisterhood. I was five for Christ's sake. Forgive me.

## When I turned fourteen, my mother's sister took me to lunch and said:

*(A Sister Poem)*

soon you'll have breasts. They'll mushroom
on your smooth chest like land mines.

A boy will show up, a schoolmate, or the gardener's son.
Pole-cat around you. All brown-eyed persistence.

He'll be everything your parents hate, a smart aleck,
a drop out, a street racer on the midnight prowl.

Even your best friend will call him a loser.
But this boy will steal your reason, have you

writing his name inside a scarlet heart, entwined
with misplaced passion and a bungled first kiss.

He'll bivouac beneath your window, sweet-talk you
until you sneak out into his waiting complications.

Go ahead, tempt him with your new-found glamour.
Tumble into the backseat of his Ford at the top of Mulholland,

flushed with stardust, his mouth in a death-clamp on your nipple,
his worshipful fingers scatting sacraments on your clit.

Soon he will deceive you with your younger sister,
the girl who once loved you most in the world.

*"Self-Portrait #2" 2011*

## when your mother convinces you to take in your homeless younger sister...

*(A Sister Poem)*

She will date your boyfriend.
She'll do it better than you ever did.
She'll have nothing but time.
He'll start showing up when you leave,
train her to make him the perfect BLT,
(crusts off, avocado on the side),
encourage his cheating heart,
suck his dick so good he'll think
he's died and gone to Jesus.

Your sister will borrow your clothes,
and look better in them than you ever did.
Someone will see her with your boyfriend
at the Grove, agonize for days
before deciding not to tell you.
Meanwhile he'll buy her that fedora
you admired in Nordstrom's window, the last one
in your size.

When you complain, your mother
will tell you it's about time you learned to share.

While you're at work, your sister will tend your garden,
weed the daisies, coax your gardenias into bloom.
No matter how many times you remind her,
she will one day forget to lock the gate;
your cat and your lawn chairs will disappear.

Your mother will say it serves you right.

Your sister will move into your boyfriend's
big house in Laurel Canyon. He will ignore her,
and she will make a half-hearted suicide attempt;
you'll rescue her once again.
Your mother will wash her hands of the pair of you,
then get cancer and die.

Smell the white gardenias in the yard.
Cherish their heady perfume. Float them in a crystal bowl.
Forgive your sister as she has forgiven you.

# Family Tree

*(A Sister Poem)*

My younger sister
climbs my limbs, steals my clothes,

sleeps at the foot of my bed,
calls it worship.

She wants the gold locket between
my breasts. She wants my breasts.

She wants my life.
It's been crowded since the day she arrived.

The slut who is my younger sister
shinnies up my tree, clambers my branches,

straddles my limbs.

She inserts herself into my conversations,
seduces my best friend,

eats my dessert.

This Mata Hari likes to watch

*(his tongue down my throat*
*hand up my skirt in the bedroom)*

spills to our parents my every sin,
calls it reverence.

And my first love?
She covets him, too.

One day she'll chop me down
to reach him.

# Boy Toy/Learning to Share

*(A Sister Poem)*


I stood in the doorway and watched Davy fuck my sister by candlelight (he never fucked me by candlelight). Their shadows conjoined, elegant. I was touching myself under my robe when they saw me. Two against one, I turned down the hall, turned down a threesome again. I'd brought him home because he talked like Davy Jones. I'd always wanted to fuck Davy Jones. So I let him be British all over me. An Anglophile, my roommate younger sister blossomed like a petunia. I thought I was learning to share. But that last night, when the sirens raged and the dogs howled in the dark, when love had me (suddenly) by the throat and my sister swore she could take him or leave him, how could I ever believe her? Anything I wanted, she wanted. So when he ping-ponged between her bed and mine, I told Davy to wear a condom. I told him I didn't know where she'd been. And when I finally begged Davy to make a choice, I watched his face carefully, ignored the implications of his sigh. *She's beautiful, your sister,* Davy said as he stroked my thigh.

# Roman Holiday

*(A Sister Poem)*

*Pino has the tiniest dick in Europe.*
My sister's thumb and forefinger
are a scant inch apart.

When it comes to postmortems,
she's worse than a man.

We stroll Villa Borghese like lovers.
The air reeks of jasmine.
We have just viewed the Caravaggios,
and are drunk on art and our own power.

This summer we've been screwing
our way through Europe,
a Brit, a Dane, two Spaniards, an Austrian
record producer, and a set of tri-lingual
Croatian twins.

Even the Texans we hooked up with near
the Spanish Steps stood no chance.

The tall blond boy & my sister, getting
sexy in the back of the restaurant;
me & the dark one, reckless,
his thick hand on my thigh.

Next week we'll move on to the Florentines,
(lecherous, slick) and we will treat more men badly,
one city as good as another,
cutting a swath of calculated payback
for every man who ever broke our hearts.

*When you're this beautiful,* my sister says,
*it's always a race against time.*

# Double Date: The Quarterback, the Fullback, & the High Cost of Dinner

*(A Sister Poem)*

When the night ends, your sister will
kiss the fullback goodnight on tip toe
under the porch light, her soft curls a halo
illuminating her naivety.

You, on the other hand,
will stare at your bare feet.
Not shy. Sullied. Seething.

Your sister will thank the fullback for dinner
at Tony's on the Pier,
the copious cocktails and signature chocolate mousse.
She'll tell him she had a wonderful time.
That she hopes she'll see him again.

You will say none of these things.
You will mind your manners.
You will try not to think how the quarterback
forced himself into your mouth.

You will bite your tongue and smile,
pretend his baller body
hasn't just slammed into yours,
like he didn't wipe his penis on your sheets
when he was done,

that while he was assaulting you,
you didn't wonder if the fullback was out there,
raping your sister. If he, too, was brutal.

In fact, your sister and the fullback only
watched TV, making out, but just a little.

You had no way to know this.

You lay there and took it for your sister.
You thought about her delicate spine,
believing if you played it wrong,
he might snap her like a sparrow.

They eyed the closed door of your bedroom.

They shared a knowing smile.
They knew nothing.

# Playing Dirty

*(A Sister Poem)*

*Your breasts are your best part,* Leonard says.

I peel off my shirt, unhook my bra,
let him feel me up in the kitchen. My sister's sleeping in.

On the fridge, a photo: Leonard in a Speedo with an obvious erection,
an arm around us both. I'm staring at the camera.

They're staring at each other.

It's pathetic to flirt, half naked, with a man who doesn't love you.
Especially if he loves your sister.

I do it anyway.

By the time she wakes up, my shirt's back on.
Leonard is doing tai chi on the terrace.

Even in daylight, he gleams like a star.

*Just this once,* my sister pleads, *let me win.*
I'm tempted to be merciful, but why start now?

Instead, that night, a threesome.

The two of us quake in Leonard's orbit,
glitter in his castoff,

we're linked like galaxies,
till he walks away from us both.

*"6th St. Loft Window Reflection"* 2015

# Casual Cruelty

*(A Sister Poem)*

1. My sister's ex eyes me at the party. *I've always wanted to nail her,* I hear him say.
I knew that.

When I ask if she minds, my sister shrugs. *I wouldn't wish him on my worst enemy.*
I take it for consent.

2. In bed, 4 a.m., my neighbor's car alarm goes off like clockwork. I can't
get back to sleep. *You want me to key her ride?* the ex asks.

He takes me to breakfast on the San Pedro pier, inspects the faded eateries,
says *they're tearing it all down.* This is the year he's investing in restaurants.

3. 'Mr. Results', he calls himself, nailing eviction notices to the rotting
wood façades. He plans on making a killing.

I ask my sister why they broke up? He's got a big cock. Nice teeth.
And an endgame. *You don't know him like I do,* she says.

4. *I've always thought you were the prettier one,* the ex tells me over dinner.
*Does my sister know?* I ask.

He shakes his head. *I'll tell her if you want me to.*
Part of me wants him to.

5. When I ask 'Mr. Results' what he's looking for, he looks right through me.
*Tell me what I'm doing wrong?* I beg.

He says he despises weakness. When he doesn't call,
I tell myself he's busy buying restaurants.

6. *You really are the more attractive one,* he says before he dumps me.
Don't tell my sister, I say at last.

*Showing mercy kind of goes against the grain, don't you think?*
He flashes that toothy grin.

7. When he throws me on the bed for old time's sake, I grit my teeth.
*Really, I mean it. Don't tell her.* But he picks up the phone.

# Poem for Formerly Amish Leonard

*(A Sister Poem)*

Your sister will accompany Leonard on road trips,
straddle him from behind the Harley he traded for his clip-clop buggy,
whisper salacious Bible verses in his ear.

She'll tell him as a girl she'd always longed to be Amish.
How she adored those high-necked, muslin convictions and chic bonnets.
How she'd long felt a religious conversion coming on.

She's always been a zealot.

Your sister will dub him a work in progress, ask Leonard to share
the beach house in Venice, with its exorbitant rent and clogged drains.

Leonard, while no virgin, will have never had *deux soeurs, en même temps*.
Not yet, anyway. The sex will be especially hot.

Each morning Leonard will make blueberry pancakes, wash the dishes,
read Tom Robbins aloud.

The three of you will spend long days on the beach,
shooting selfies as proof of life.

Each night you and your sister will compete for his affection.
It will almost come to blows.

Soon, your sister will cut you out of that photo on Venice Beach,
although your arm will still be visible around Leonard's (naked) shoulder.
Then she'll do her best to cut you out of his life.

In the end, Leonard will flee your squabbling for the open road,
his long-haired freedom billowing out behind him,
careening toward countless women yet to be conquered,

and as far away from the two of you as he can get.

# Survivor's Guilt

*(A Sister Poem)*

*—After childhood trauma from* The Pawnbroker, The Night Porter,
      The Third Man, *& other disturbing films.*

Would the Nazis have killed me outright or used me for labor or sex?
This has always been the litmus test.

When I was young I knew the answer, but now I know it too,
and it is a different answer.

I'd thought myself worthy of cruel experiments, or saved from slaughter
by a sadistic, SS officer who wanted just to fuck me, but found me addictive.

*"Fucking" doesn't shock anymore,* my sister said when she read the poem.
*True,* I agreed. *But "genocide"* does.

I imagined my fragile sister, naked in the mis-named queue labeled
*"SHOWERS."*

When I visited the Anne Frank House in Amsterdam,
I was struck by the fear that still clung to those rooms.

I followed Anne up the tiny stairs behind the bookcase,
their claustrophobic chaos, the lingering anticipation

of her bedroom. Anne's winsome spirit welcomed me in:
kept as it was when the Nazis came, movie star photos

still taped to her walls.

## Birthday Girl Blues at Philippe's "the Original" French Dip Sandwich in L.A.

*(A Sister Poem)*

*Happy Birthday!* My sister, newly sober, lifts her coffee cup. I want to tear the birthday greetings off the wall, stomp the fast-deflating mylar balloons, rip the cardboard tiara from my head. Instead, I bite my tongue, toy with my apple pie. *Remember your 21st? Right here, baby.* My sister pounds the table. Glitter stars jump and scatter, mingle with the sawdust on the floor. If you'd told me then I'd be here now, I'd have called you a liar. If you'd told me then she'd be here with me, I'd have shot myself. I stare at the two empty seats at the table, coffee cups untouched. *I swear on mom's grave I invited them!* my sister says. I don't know who she's talking about. It's closing time. Ours, the only un-bussed table. Crusts, abandoned on our plates, the au jus cold in the bowl. My sister could almost pass for twenty in this light; then to now is a blur, a stumble, a montage of our regrets. My sister reaches across the table, but I won't take her hand. Too much water under the bridge. She smiles at me like she loves me. *Forty sucks, anyway you cut it,* my sister says.

Night spills through the diner windows, blocking out the future, closing in on the past. I see my sister's fat reflection. I'm afraid to look at my own.

*"Black Bart Knife Thrower Extraordinaire"* 2016

# Leash

*"You dangle on the leash of your own longing; your need grows teeth."*
— Margaret Atwood

She was his ideal.
He was a rescue.
She saw potential. He saw stars.

They were destined, those two.
God-like, everyone agreed,
their own edgy breed.

(We all wanted to be them.)

At the wedding, his dog ran circles,
lashed its leash around the two of them
like fate.

He and the dog were a package deal.
Not that she minded.
Was it the novelty?

He was easy. She dug in her heels.
She had a plan: He'd give up everything.
And like it.

The townhouse, the baby.
Idyllic. Until what?
The long haul? Ennui?

Define *rough patch* I longed to ask
when he told me they'd split.
Did he stray? Did she want too much?

The two of them, mum, dangling.
Me? I can't sleep
for pondering the mystery.

# Divorce & Mass Shootings in the Time of Trump

She wants a divorce, flips a coin for the cat, kisses you goodbye.
The usual mixed message.

*You pay for dinner, and I'll pay attention,* she'd laugh when you two were dating.
You thought it was a joke but now you know better.

*Why are there no straight lines from you to anywhere?*
your wife cries from behind the steering wheel of the Beemer.

You know the answer: Everything's shifting. It's all a façade.
*Vegas is a desert,* you warn. *Built on sand.* But she drives off anyway.

No one loves anyone anymore.

The bedsheets smell like your wife. You pull them over your head.
When you think of her, your stomach snakes.

*I'm too old to start over,* you complain to your Facebook friends.
For company you buy a new cat, and a rifle.

You wake to the next mass shooting. This time Las Vegas.
Why not call it *The Mandalay Bay Massacre?* you ask the cat.

Or the *Country Music Catastrophe?* the cat answers.
All those music fans, doomed as lovers in a country song.

The divorce papers arrive via messenger. Your wife wants everything.
The cat laughs. *Of course she does!*

No one listens to reason anymore, why should you?

Enough days without her, shut in with the cat and an M-16, and
you understand the mindset of the mass shooter:

If you buy a gun you must learn to shoot it.
You almost have to shoot it.

*(for Leo Kolp)*

## Lust at the Cafe Formosa

Once, at the Cafe Formosa in L.A.,
I saw the most beautiful girl. And the best part was,
you could see she didn't know it. Yet.
Didn't know how anxiously her nipples strained
against her shirt, or that her endless legs
and sloe-eyed gaze were worth
a million bucks... to someone.

She was a sway-in-the-wind willow, her skin
the pale of vanilla ice cream, her hair all shiny black,
straight like an Asian girl's, thick as a mop.
She was maybe seventeen, on the brink, so ripe
sex exuded from her pores. She leaned against the juke box
fingering those quarters in her shorts' pocket
so they jingled like Christmas, the fabric between
her thighs stretched to bursting.

When her food arrived, the girl unwrapped
the chopsticks, lifted Kung Pow chicken to her mouth,
inhaled the spicy morsels. A long, sauce-slicked
noodle played with her lips and I longed to lick it off.
I'd been alone four years by then,
so used to it even the longing had long departed.

Then she showed up, all fresh-spangled, clueless.
If I didn't walk out then I never would. Elvis
was crooning *Don't Be Cruel,* but I knew she would be.
Girls like her can't help it.

# White Flag

*On Edward Hopper's painting, "Morning Sun," 1952*

No one paints loneliness like he does. Those half-clad women by the bed, on the floor, hunched over, staring out the window, in profile or from behind, always clean lines, such worshipful light. The gas station in the middle of nowhere, estranged couples on the bright-lit porch after dark. Even the boats sail alone. And the diners. The hatted strangers, coming on to a redhead, a moody blonde, all of them losers, all of them desperate for a second chance. This morning the sunlight pried open my eyes, flooded our bedroom walls. I sat alone, in profile on our bed in a pink chemise, knees drawn up, arms crossed over my calves, staring out the window. Desperate for you. No one paints loneliness like Edward Hopper paints me, missing you, apologies on my lips. Come back. Stand below my window. Watch me beg for a second chance. Downturned mouth, sad eyes, parted knees, open thighs, that famous shaft of Hopper light a white flag, if only you could see.

*"Pawn Shop, Pacific St. San Pedro"* 2019

# Walk All over You

The stiletto boots in the back of my closet
are restless, long to stroll the 3rd Street Promenade,
looking for a red silk bustier. A Louis Vuitton bag.
A lover who won't let me down.

The stiletto boots in the back of my closet
want to party, want to grab my feet,
climb my calves, hug my thighs. They're
ready for action. Ready to put on a skintight
Versace. Ready to head for the club.

They want to clack on terrazzo floors,
totter from great heights, see the world.
Escape the flats, the Mary Jane's, the penny
loafers, the two-toned, two-faced saddle Oxfords
that guard the closet door.

The stiletto boots in the back of my closet
want to walk all over you, punish you
for cheating, make you pay.
They long to wrap themselves around
you, put you in a headlock, rake your thighs—
want to lead you into

Debauchery.
Saran Wrap.
Whipped cream.
Wesson Oil.
Room service.

Remember?

The stiletto boots have a short attention span, choose
not to remember why they were banished, or what
you did. They're desperate to reclaim you,
dig their heels into your shortcomings,
make little marks up and down your libido.
Welcome you home.

My stilettos can't forget you.
My stilettos can't move on.
My stilettos will forgive you.
Even if I cannot.

They bear the scuff marks
of your betrayal far better than do I.

Like the last time and the time before.
They want to get started, head out the door.
Who do you think gave me those fucking boots,
anyway?

# His Full Attention

Eduardo's exceptionally large. When he drives too fast up the mountain, yanking me to him on the curves, his body is an invitation. I keep my eyes on the road, a silver ribbon, illuminated by the full moon. *"Eres una chica,"* Eduardo croons, his thick, right arm over my shoulder, his left hand on the wheel. *Can I really play a tough girl?* I think, and run my fingers lightly over his warm, brown skin, twirl the lock of wavy black hair that keeps falling into his eyes.

When we reach the summit, he parks the Chrysler and lets the top down, turns up the CD player. Vintage Selena, the song about falling. He sings along, *Siempre estoy sonando en ti.*

The night settles around us like anesthesia. Past the car is no-man's land, the fog's soft deception a trompe l'oeil, like we could exit the car, leap beyond the mountain's edge and trust the clouds to catch us. I stare into the blackness, beyond where the road dead ends into a cottony cloud. *"Es mysterioso, la niebla,"* Eduardo says, pulling me closer.

*You hardly know him!* My mother's voice is loud in my ear. But that's the point. Some random pickup from La Habra, a place I'd never been before and never would again. A man I'd never run into after tonight. *Not our kind,* my grandmother would say. *Slumming,* my girlfriends call it. *Exactly.* A bit of harmless fun, just how I dreamed it. Maybe he'll even give me a Spanish lesson.

I am newly seventeen, sick to death of my vanilla life, my womanhood a bravado with no foundation. So when Eduardo kisses me, I open my mouth. When he puts his hands on my breasts I help him take off my sweater. I've fantasized this moment for years, hot sex with some dark, silent stranger who knows how to touch me. All action. No talk, unlike the pale, timid boys I know. But my adolescence, a steady diet of G-rated Hollywood romantic comedies where everything stays above the waist, has me ill-prepared. When Eduardo undoes the brass button of my jeans, unzipping them in one, practiced movement, when his huge middle finger finds its way between my thighs, I'm caught somewhere between heaven and the top of Topanga.

I have not come here for the conversation, my maid-taught, kitchen Spanish, and Eduardo's fledgling *Inglés* was already exhausted over dinner. So when he pushes the lever and the seats ease back in the Chrysler I shimmy out of my jeans. Eduardo sheds his pants, covers my body with his. He smells of citrus and the freshly ironed shirt I unbutton, my fingers clumsy with desire. He probes my mouth with his tongue, licking, exploring, his hands on my breasts, the weight of his body pressed against me, a welcome pleasure.

*So this is sex,* I think as Eduardo parts my thighs. I have not told him I am a virgin. Still, I soon like it, the rhythmic in and out, the way he fits into me, how I have his full attention. I match his breathing, bring my hips up to meet him. *I'm a natural,* I think as his fingers on my clit make me come. Then Eduardo pulls out his cock, spasms all over my belly.

After it's over, I look skyward, watch the moon slip in and out of the clouds. It's deathly quiet. Only the sound of Selena's sad singing.

I struggle to sit up, but Eduardo pins me down, his hands encircling my wrists. He is looking at me oddly, like he's surprised to see me there, underneath him, like he's never seen me before. His dark hair is disheveled, strands stuck to his forehead.

"Let me up," I tell him. But he won't. Instead, he peers into my face.

"Why you come up here? Why you do this?" he asks. "You are *loca?*" He looks down at me. Crazy? No. Adventurous. Headstrong, maybe.

He cradles my head, strokes my hair, gently at first, then more roughly, his fingers twisting the blonde strands. "You like *exótico?*" Eduardo sounds more like a cop than a lover. "You like *los hombres oscuros? ¿Peligro?*" I'm trying to understand. Danger? No, fun and games. Now take me home! But Eduardo has other plans.

His hand covers my breast. Squeezes. "You like it rough, *señorita?* Is this what you expect from a man like me?" His breathing is harsh, ragged as he opens the Chrysler door. *"¿Tienes ganas de morir?"*

Death wish? No. How can I explain slumming? That I meant no harm? That we each got what we came for, didn't we?

"Eduardo," I begin, but he pulls me naked from the car, urges me toward the precipice. I don't want to go. I remember the words, *"Llévame a casa!"* But there's something he wants me to see.

*"Mira!"* he points to the cloud bank below. "Look!" he says. "You think you dive in, the clouds they will hold you? *¿No caería?"* I would not fall. I tell him again that I want to go home, but instead he holds me closer, inches us toward the edge. He's still humming that Selena song about falling. *"Podría caer."* I could fall.

The mist is a shhh! around my ears. "Fall in love, I could fall in love…" he's singing. I make out a word here and there.

Eduardo embraces me, and we're dancing, his arms a vise as he maneuvers me toward oblivion. Then the Spanish lesson begins:

*Nadie llega hasta aquí.* No one comes here.

*Podría matarte.* I could kill you.

*Yo podría empujar sobre el borde.* I could push you over the edge. Eduardo grips my shoulders. I have never felt this alive.

*No tengas miedo!* Don't be afraid!

I'm the tough girl. I'm not afraid. The cotton candy clouds swirl and plump, promise a soft landing. And I won't be going down alone.

I clutch his arms, dig my nails into his skin. *Piel,* I remember. *Piel moreno.* Such beautiful brown skin.

# Caged

*"Birds born in cages think that flying is an illness."* Alejandro Jodorowsky

He loves me because I look like his mother at 30.
I discover her photo in a secret drawer,
the same rounded hips,

and dark, wavy hair,
her pale, off-the-shoulder blouse an exact
duplicate of one he's given me.

She has bigger breasts, deeper cleavage.
*You eat like a bird!* her son chastises,
passing me the cheesecake.

Suddenly it all makes sense.
Like when he cries *Mama!* in his dreams.
Awakens empty-armed. Abandoned.

He does not cry for me.

Shoved under our door, a flyer:
"If you find a dead bird, call 1-877-WNV-BIRD."
Lost between the bed and the mirror, I look and look.

He hides his obsession in a stack of magazines
in the bathroom. A blur of a girl, naked,
disappearing in a doorway. It could be his mother.

He locks the door.

Plump bird. Feathered nest.
Force-fed. *Fois gras.*
Fattened up for slaughter.

Someone's dinner. Someone's daughter.

When he hits me because I look like his mother,
he pulls back his fist, takes aim at her caged facsimile.
I hold perfectly still.

We both know he could never hit his mother.

# Property

**1. In the light**
I keep thinking about the way
you keep your thumb hooked
in the belt loop of my jeans,
like you have me on a leash,
like you own me.
I'm not sure I don't like it.

**2. In the dark**
I lie on top, your skin grazes mine.
I breathe your scent, burrow in your flesh,
forehead flush against your belly,
eager mouth fellating your cock.
So this is love!

**3. In the even darker**
Go ahead. Push me down.
Pin my wrists.
Wedge your knees between my thighs;
pry me open. You know
you want to explore my corridor,
my antechamber,
my presidential suite. There's a basket
of fruit on my D-cup titties,
Veuve Clicquot in my 'fridge.

**4. In the winter**
You like fucking on top of the sheets,
heater off, windows open
to remind us we're still breathing.
I can see your breath,
its smoke—and mirrors.

**5. In the cut**
I keep thinking about the way
you keep me under your thumb.
"Yes," you say. "This is love."
And I'm not sure I don't like it.

*"Waitress & Busboy, The Artisan House, DTLA"* 2016

# Murakami Cento Love Poem #1

*All text taken from Haruki Murakami's,* Norwegian Wood.

1.
It rained on her birthday.

2.
I could feel the soft swell of her breasts on my chest.

She herself had become small and narrow.
*Don't worry,* I said. *Just relax.*

Before I knew it, I was kissing her.

Her breathing intensified and her throat began to tremble.
I parted her long, slim legs.

*But I'm scared,* she said.

She seemed to be turning over something in her mind.

*Do you have a girl you like?* she asked.

I took a sip of wine, as if I had never heard anything.

3.
We were alive, she and I.

I moved my lips up her neck to her ear and took a nipple
with the finger of my other hand.

We explored each other's bodies in the darkness without words.

It was easy. Almost too easy.

4.
Glass shattered somewhere.
I felt no pain to speak of, but the blood wouldn't stop.

5.
I smelled the meadow grass, heard the rain at night.

6.
It was easy to tell which room was hers.
All I had to do was find the one window toward the back
where a faint light trembled.

*Come in,* she said.

# Murakami Cento Love Poem #2

*All text taken from Haruki Murakami's,* Norwegian Wood.
*(Those were strange days, now that I look back at them.)*


1.
*Things are not going well at home,* she said.
She had slimmed down, as if she had been
hiding in some long, narrow space.
Clouds of black smoke shot up and flowed
with the breeze out toward the main street.
*I'm not sure that has anything to do with love,* I said.

2.
Wildly chopped, her hair stuck out in patches
and the bands lay crooked against her forehead,
but the style suited her.

3.
We drank and watched the black smoke rising.
A burning smell filled the air.

*It's true. Don't you think I'm terrible? Cold-hearted?*
I didn't feel anything.

4.
I was always hungry for love.
She must have been exhausted.

5.
*Do you love me? Will you remember that I existed?*
I returned to that small world of hers.
I could feel the outline of her body in my hands.
*Always,* I said. *I'll always remember.*

6.
I still don't know why she chose me.

7.
What could have kept burning so long?

*Anyhow,* she said, *let's stay here and watch for a while.*
*And if something bad happens, we can think about it then.*

8.
The wind started shifting unpredictably, and
white ash flakes fell out of the air around us.

I fell into the kind of deep sleep I had not had for a long time;

9.
Nothing but snow... and more snow everywhere you looked.

# Murakami Cento Love Poem #3

*All text taken from Haruki Murakami's,* Norwegian Wood

1.
Sunlight stabbed my eyes, mouth coated with sand,
head belonging to someone else.

2.
A short silence followed.
I stared for a long time at her naked shoulder.

And it hurt so much, I didn't know what to do.
But even so, I never told her.

Something was gone now and I was
probably the one who had destroyed it.

*I'll never forget you,* I said.

3.
She kept apologizing in this pitiful voice
like she was really sorry,
and I kept telling her *it's O.K., it's O.K.*

4.
*I don't want to get you involved in my sexual fantasies,* she said.
Pressed against me, her whole body trembling,
she continued to cry.

5.
I slept with her that night.

She made it clear that she wanted me to give her release.
It sent a thrill through me when she did that—a nice thrill.

I kissed her.
She clutched at my erection.
Her cry was the saddest sound of orgasm I had ever heard.

# I Prefer Pussy (a little city-kitty ditty)

I prefer pussy, as in cat
as in willow
as in chases a rat
as in raised on a pillow.

I prefer pussy, as in riot
as in foots
as in pussycat doll
as in puss-in-boots.

I prefer pussy, as a twat
it is not, nor
is it a beaver,
a clam or a cleaver.

I prefer pussy to
nookie or gash,
it isn't a box,
or a cave or a slash.

I prefer pussy, 'though
rosebud's not bad,
and muffin sounds homey,
and cooch makes me glad.

I prefer pussy to snapper
or snatch, far better
than taco or
slit or man-catch.

I prefer pussy, as in whip
as in flower,
as into it you slip—
as in *I* have the power.

*"Self-Portrait #3" 2012*

# Morning Wood

"Touch it," he says.

My lips graze the tip.

His penis tastes
like sleep.

In his
hips'
hollow,

between
his pincer
thighs, I nestle.

Open-windowed
sunlight
climbs the walls,

honeys his dear
face.

I long to inhabit him.

"Do you think
of your penis

as an 'It'
or a 'He'?"

"Neither," he says.
"I think of it as 'Me'."

# Below our bedroom window

the gardeners are cutting down the giant yucca tree with a chainsaw, while inside, we have sex. It's a turn on, one man inside me, and two outside, silhouetted against the vertical blind; it makes me even louder than usual. But my moans are obliterated by the chainsaw's guttural wail, mixed with the gardeners' chatter, as they sever the yucca's limbs. Twin brothers, the gardeners arrive bi-weekly to manicure the grass, trim the hedges. They're identical, stocky, bearded. Muscles ripple their shirts. Tools hang from their utility belts, sagging their jeans. I say hello when we cross paths, feel the warmth of their smiles. I imagine them now, twin faces against the glass, peering through a space in the slats, made aware of me in *deshabille,* a crimson corset winnowing my waist, pale-nippled breasts overflowing the cups. It's hot, and I've pinned my black hair atop my head, loose tendrils trailing down my sweaty neck.

Who told them to murder the yucca? Its spiked leaves hid our daytime exploits, bedroom window open to the breeze. Gone, we stifle. *But an open window,* my lover cautions, *is a voyeur's carte blanche.* Would those two spy on him, nibbling me, his face between my lace garters? *I like you accessible,* my lover says. I wonder, would the twins like that, too? Afterward, I rush to the window to view the carnage. The brothers long gone. The yucca, in pieces, spilling sap, mirrors the trickle down my inner thighs.

## Accidental Lover

This is no accident.

Feelings are involved, dammit.
Bodily injury. Emotional distress.

In the oncoming rhapsody of her headlights, you
see your sixth birthday, the bumper cars.

When you connect, your tape-looped
head smashes against the windshield.

Don't be surprised when the paramedics
pull the sheet over your face.

Your sweet mama's ghost
will shine a light.

Aim for the high beams,
the blindside;

focus on her final release.

Revel in the impact,
the ephemera of Truth,
the hard fast pleasure in
shifting
down.

# Gold Star Lesbian

Once, in a moment of recklessness, I fell in love with Phoebe, an older, yet still delicious lipstick lesbian, who swore she would spoil me for any man. My first ex-husband was shacked up with my ex-best friend; husband #2 was lurking, just around the corner. It was a window. Phoebe, a buyer for Bullocks Wilshire, that art deco building gleaming on Miracle Mile, used her employee discount to clothe me in style, bought me silk blouses, linen trousers, tailored suits. She liked her women sleek. Understated. Wild hair tamed into a lacquered updo, secured with antique Japanese combs. I was a whole new me. Squelched. Ladylike, but for the four inch stilettos and the fushia corset sequestered inside my high-buttoned faux-modesty. I reveled in how it arched my back, my breasts thrust forward, an offering. Phoebe liked it, too. She'd trace the corset stays encircling my ribs with her index finger, her eyes glued to mine like Mesmer. Underneath all that polish and restraint beat a frenzied heart. You would not believe how fast that tailored suit hit the floor, stilettos kicked off like a pesky persona. She was a Gold Star lesbian, untouched by men, although plenty must have pursued her, her golden hair and haughty beauty an irresistible lure. I was all in, worshipful; I followed Phoebe around like a dog. She swore she'd been alone for years, that I was her re-awakening, that no one had ever made her come so good. But that night, at her favorite club, the fresh graffiti on the toilet stall wall told a different story:

> Phoebe
> has the
> most pleasurable
> vagina this side
> of Saturn except
> 4 your mom

99

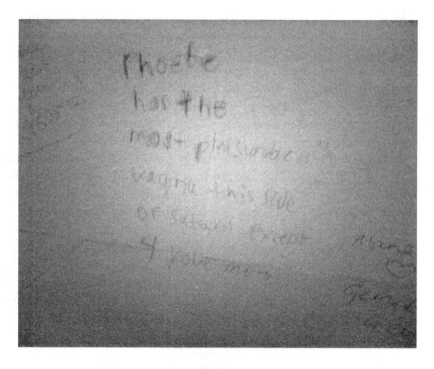

*"Phoebe's Vagina, Ladies Room Stall, Green Mill Bar, Chicago" 2008*

## When I Turned Sixteen Mother Let Uncle Kenny from Chicago Take Me for a Ride

1. Uncle Kenny let the top down on the Chrysler,
fedora protecting his tender scalp.

When I got into the car
he threw his arm over the bucket seat,
fingers grazing the back of my skimpy tube top.

2. PCH, left on Sunset, he took Deadman's Curve
like a pro, then the slow cruise
to downtown. Like he'd been here before.

July baked my bare shoulders.
Like Uncle Kenny, I burned easily.

3. Sunset ended at Olivera Street.
My uncle chose La Golondrina Cafe.
I ordered the cheese enchiladas.
He ordered a double Margarita, extra salt.

Things I Learned At Lunch:
Dress Well.
Travel Light.
Marry Up.

*My mom says you're good for nothing,* I said.

Uncle Kenny slid so close in the booth
his trousers tickled my thigh.

*I once made love to Hedy Lamar,*
he confessed.

He ran his tongue around the rim of
the margarita glass, licked the salt.
His blue eyes stared right past me.

When the mariachis reached
our table, Uncle Kenny pulled me from the booth,
spun me around the restaurant.

Like all big men, he was light on his feet.

4. The overpriced gold and ruby chandelier earrings
serenaded us from the store window.

5. *How much damage,* my mother reasoned,
*can he do my girl in one afternoon?*

6. When Uncle Kenny died soon after
in flagrante delicto, no one was surprised.

*I heard it was his heart,* my mother said,
*but I know he didn't have one.*

She clipped his obituary out of the paper,
pinned it to the refrigerator with a magnet.

In *my* heart I knew differently.

I drove PCH north, left on Sunset,
an Uncle Kennyesque fedora
shading my eyes.

At Dead Man's Curve
I threw my head back like I'd seen
Hedy Lamar do in the movies.

My chandelier earrings tinkled in the wind.

# (Menage a Trois) Tonight I Dream of My First True Love

*"Trembling, like Paris, on the brink of an obscure and formidable revolution."*
—Victor Hugo

It feels like a competition. I lay between the two of them, sweltering, like Paris in August. Gene's lanky six foot four inches hangs off the foot of the bed, Brett's dancer-body liquid, compact, is curled into mine, his hard need pressed against my thigh. I'm not sure how I ended up here, in love with a man who wants me to fuck his best friend while he watches. Now the three of us crowd in my too-small bed. I stare at a black and white photo of Montmartre on the ceiling. Brett trembles like needle to the pole. Van Morrison's on the radio, having sex in the green grass with the brown-eyed girl. The ceiling fan rotates counterclockwise, but we're all sweating. I should have moved the beds together when my roommate moved out, but it's too late, now Gene's spread my thighs, and pinned his best friend against the wall, and now he says nothing while Brett watches him slam into me. I need him to scream *I love you!* again and again like he did before. But Gene's eyes are locked with Brett's. I see what I'm not meant to see; I am disposable, nothing more than a deep hole. A hot rain pelts the bedroom window. Gene pours into me like runoff. His tears look like raindrops on glass. I turn his face so he can see what he is losing. I want him to watch his best friend as he arches his dancer's back and comes in my mouth, his spasms an arabesque. I pull back my hair and dip my head, *trembling, like Paris, on the brink of an obscure and formidable revolution.*

## When the Handsome, Overgrown Samoan Boy Stands Again in Front of Your Glass-Walled Beach House in Venice & Begins to Masturbate, Never Taking His Eyes off You...

Lock eyes with your accomplice.

This is what comes with glass houses.

He will touch himself through denim.
His dick will break free of his cut-off jeans,

Bigger than a cucumber.

Don't worry! His eyes will never leave your face.
No one will guess your truth.

Reach under your skirt, pull aside your panties,
Touch your rock hard clit.

Watch your reflection in the window glass as
Daylight shifts into dusk,

Look at his face as you make yourself come.

This is how you cope with loss.

# Spreading My Legs for Someone (Posing for Pirelli)

The grey-suited Pirelli rep. sat behind the desk,
puffing on a cigarette. White smoke hung in the air
like surrender.
I slipped off my dress.
Kept my stilettos.

There was nothing on the agency man's glass-topped
brain but my nakedness.
He wouldn't meet my eye.

"Jesus!" he exclaimed when I bent over
to tighten an ankle strap.

The photographer looked like Antonio Banderas.
"Sit down on the seamless," he said, pointing
to the black backdrop that spilled onto the floor.

He rolled the tire over to me, snapped on the lights.
I sat, cross-legged, clutching the tire close.

My naked breasts peeked through the center,
the nipples erect. I laid my hot face along the tread.

The photographer pushed up his cashmere sleeves,
picked up his Nikon.

The lights bore down like August; the cement
below the seamless bruised my ass. The two men
stared at me the way my stepfather did.

I pushed the damp strands of hair from my forehead.
Arched my back. Opened my thighs.

The suit lit another cigarette.
Antonio Banderas moved in for a close-up.

"Is this what you want?" I asked.

My feet poked out from the tire's rubber frame
like destiny.

*"Waitress, The Artisan House, DTLA"* 2016

# Love Song for My Baby

If I could catch my breath I'd suck your cock but I'm so overcome by your studly chest, your hairy thighs, your endearingly bony knees that I'm afraid I'd choke on it. Anyway, forget the preliminaries, I just want to jump your bones, throw a saddle over your rump and ride, pony, ride. I want to blog on your biceps, write erotica on your elbows, I want to tattoo my memoirs on your ass. I want to lead you out of the stable, trot you around, give you your head, then rein you in. I want you to taste the bit in your mouth, and have it taste sweet like Tic Tacs, like summer time, like ginger-ale. Just like you taste to me. I want to corral you in my arms, cavort in the moonlight, dos si dos with the best of 'em. I could put you on the stage in Tijuana. That donkey's dick's got nothing on you, babe. *Nada. Niet. Rien.* My very own John Holmes. I woke yesterday in a pool of you and me. Your lips fastened on my pussy, your hot breath steaming up my thighs. You were humming the theme from Dr. Zhivago and the dark buzz made my clitty hard like a little dick. So kiss me already, and then let's stick it in, this is L.A. for Chrissakes, and the livin' is on the beach, on the fly, on the installment plan. Do ya wanna know how I see it? Each of us teeters on the totter, a paycheck away from homeless, from ruin, just one pitch away from a shutout, one sweet fuck away from the end.

## Your Target

The last man I fucked before my husband
is standing in the shampoo aisle at my local Target
when our carts collide. He's not surprised to see me.

"I knew I would find you here," he says
in that French accent I once found irresistible. "After all,
this is *your* Target." He pronounces it like
it's some high-end sex boutique instead of Walmart
with better commercials.

I spent three years in his bed. I brought the pussy.
He supplied the passion and the pot. He had the biggest
cock I'd seen, and if size had been the measure
of a relationship, we'd never have parted.

How do you tell your ex that he opened you up,
made you ripe for the one true love who followed?

The last man I fucked before my husband grabs my hand,
brings it to his lips. "I heard you were married?" he asks,
a flicker of hope in his eyes. I nod; he sighs.

"When I taught you how to love again," he says. "I thought
you would love me."

## Tonight I Dream of My Last Meal with My First Ex-Husband Who Was Both Fickle & Bent

There was yet another threesome on the menu. Him, the platinum divorcée from next door, and that TV actress who followed me home. A triple-decker; blonde on blonde on blonde. Hold the mayo. I knew they'd hit it off. Like replacement china. Each of them chipped someplace marginal. I admit to damaged, self-besotted, brunette. When I married him I thought: *I will divorce you in a year.* What was *he* thinking? He used to tie me to the bed posts—the only way he could get off. I didn't mind. He hated that. When the shenanigans paled, and his money ran out, I wanted out. Was that when he decided to keep me, *and* the TV actress, *and* the platinum blonde? Never could make up his mind. His dick (did I mention?) was slanted to the left, like his politics. A girl could get addicted to that bit of kink.

## Tonight I Dream of My Second Ex-Husband Who Played Piano Better Than Herbie Hand Cock

Naked and unperturbed, hard-on the size of an Eagle Scout's flashlight, he watches me sleep, standing at my bedside like he still lives here. Framed drawings of me, 17 and naked, hang like cautionary muses above my bed. His eyes devour them like that sweet girl still exists. Like he didn't grind her into extinction with each lie, each humiliating indiscretion. In this dream he's twenty-five, and almost sure he loves me. And then he's thirty. And then he's gone. But right now he's tonguing me from behind, (that drawing of me on all fours), my labia symmetrical, curving against my inner thighs like geometry. He fingers his cock. He looks like Wesley Snipes in *Blade*. He pinches my left nipple; his practiced mouth seeking out my complicity. Why does the fantasy always best real life? My second ex-husband sits on the edge of my dream, smoothes the hair from my forehead with his piano-widened hands. When his fingers dance arpeggios on my face it feels like foreplay. When I reach for the dildo on the nightstand, it starts itself.

# Ernest, as in Hemingway

*(After A Hot Girls' Night at Farfalla on La Brea, We Smoke A Blunt In Lynne's Lexus)*

*300 days since I'd had sex. The attractive pawnbroker behind the counter who flirted with me had no idea, when he passed me the expensive watch, that the graze of his hand set off sparks. The Cartier was an aphrodisiac; that watch had weight. Its 14K gold and stainless steel band begged to wrap itself around my wrist. I twisted my arm so the Cartier caught the pawnshop's florescent light. Two grand cash was burning a hole in my wallet. I'd hoped it was enough.*

There's a tap on the window. Lynne starts the engine. Sue's shotgun, me and Nanette in back. I stub out the joint, reluctantly roll down the window, but dude's not a cop. Late 30's, bearded, skinny white guy. Jewish, given the neighborhood. No threat. He's followed us from the bar, wants to join us, get high, so I open the door, scooch over.

He takes my hand, solemnly introduces himself to each of us. "Ernest," he says. "As in Hemingway."

"I'm a big fan of *A Farewell To Arms*," Sue jokes when he won't let go of her hand. Nanette, who bats for the other team, plays Solitaire on her phone. Our benevolent hostess breaks out another blunt. Ernest settles in, takes a hit, then another. He's rubbing against me, but not in a bad way. Says he owns a pawn shop in Hollywood. I'm in the market for a Cartier Panther. "I have one in stock," he exhales.

Next day, flirting over the pawn shop counter after the "killer deal" he's made me on the watch, an invitation. He'll make me dinner at his place. I think we have a connection. I watch Ernest tackle the coq au vin, hang on his words. He tells me I'm beautiful. We drink too much wine. Then he gives me the tour; says he's cherry-picked all the best pieces from the pawn shop for himself. A Chagall, an Eames chair and matching ottoman grace the living room. "Astonishing," Ernest says, "what folks will part with when they're desperate."

He lights the crystal chandelier over the mahogany dining table, tells me it's "Czech, prewar." He has good taste. Does *he* taste good? That's the liquor and the deprivation talking, and the Thai stick we're smoking adds to my confusion. When he kisses me I kiss him back, allow his hands to roam. Ernest unzips my jeans, reaches inside. I cum when he touches me. Love-starved.

I picture waking each morning in Ernest's white, Spanish stucco bedroom with exposed beams. I could be happy here, lucky at last! Ernest has a house, a good career, not the usual waiter/actor I'm used to bedding, back when I still believed in love. But last night, of the four women getting high in Lynne's Lexus, Ernest had chosen me. Maybe it was about more than the Cartier.

Above the headboard, an obscenely large Miro. An antique beveled mirror reflects us on the bed, and we look wanton, content. On the nightstand, sadly, Ayn Rand. But no one's perfect. I unbuckle his belt, unzip him. Fellate his small, hard cock, wonder how it will feel inside me. When he comes, Ernest does not return the favor. Instead, he zips up my jeans, walks me out.

"Enjoy the Cartier," he says as he finesses me into the car, shuts the door. When I lower the window to say goodnight, he leans in, like he's going to kiss me, ask me out again. Instead, he grips my wrist. Squeezes earnestly. "Can you text me the numbers of your three friends from last night?" he asks. "That was so hot, getting loaded in the car!" He laughs. "Help me out here," Ernest says. "I wanna do you all."

*"Deli / Liquor, Pacific St., San Pedro"* 2017

# Dear Nordstrom,

I'm returning the red velvet party dress I bought for M.'s birthday, unworn. Yes, it hugs my ass, and the fine lace inset exploits my breasts, and although it makes me feel like a vixen, the unexpected break up with my intended (for reasons I don't want to get into except to say I most certainly am divorced from my 3rd husband) make the dress irrelevant. Anyway, maybe it's best I didn't go to the party, because my friend Bambi says I'd have been way overdressed—that she was the only one in a frock, because this, after all, is California. *People showed up dressed like they were going to the laundromat or the movies!* she said, forever an East Coast girl. Her high heels sank into the soggy lawn of the backyard where refreshments were served. I could have been a refreshment myself, in red velvet, but I'd rather be naked and watching a movie. Eating red velvet cake. Or fucking. Look, if I had a nickel for every party I didn't attend I'd still bring back the dress. Nordstrom, your return policy is legendary. The tag, like my heart, is still attached.

Faithfully Yours,

## Dear Mrs. Brown, Your Husband Whimpers When He Comes...

1. "I want my wife to know all about us," he says. We're close together on the couch, but not yet touching. She needn't worry. "What is there to know? Just tell her I don't fuck married men." I see his sad face crumble. Mr. Brown hates the truth almost as much as he hates bad language. Sometimes I curse to rile him, but tonight it just comes out. We're back from dinner at Micelli's on Melrose, that lonely table in the back in the dark and so far from San Pedro no one he knows will find him. I suddenly want more out of life.

Mr. Brown pulls me to him. His tweed sports coat scratches my bare arms. I breathe in his Amphora pipe tobacco and English Leather. He smells like my dad, who never held me like this. Unused to kissing, Mr. Brown's tentative lips brush mine. I push my tongue past his teeth. His erection, a pup tent of unrequited love. Against my better judgement, I let him dry hump my thigh.

Afterward, I fix my hair at the hallway mirror while Mr. Brown fastens a locket around my neck. I can make out an "L" in bright diamonds. It is not my initial. "L?" my eyes catch his in the reflection. "For Lust," he smiles. (Or maybe L for his wife, Lucia, or L for Leaving her, I don't say.) L for Lonely. Looney. Lost, I think as Mr. Brown's hands roam my body, the shiny locket the price of admission. I stare at our mismatched reflections, the almost incestuous nature of our non-romance. I finger the Jaeger-Lecoultre Reverso watch he gave me last fall (that rough patch when he left his wife for all of a week until she threatened suicide, again). Mr. Brown showed me the texts. Before he went home, he gave me Lucia's watch. "She'll never miss it," he said as he fastened it on my wrist. She has excellent taste.

2. When I visit Mr. Brown's bedside after the quadruple bypass, I put the extravagant blue iris bouquet in a vase, perch on his hospital bed and fill him in about my fucked-up life, the flood in the kitchen, my crappy new boss. He complains about the hospital food and remarks how a heart attack can truly mess up your day. I confess how lonely I am without him. "I'm thinking of leaving my wife," he tells me. I let him feel me up. "My heart attack is a wake up call," he says. *Carpe Diem."*

On a hunch, I ask him when he's buying the red Corvette. "Blue," Mr. Brown says. "I ordered it in blue." Like the irises. Like the hospital walls. "Like the way I am without you," I admit. I'm about to ask him to take me along to pick up the new wheels, when Lucia and her friends waltz into the room. They see him, all over me, on his bed, her lost locket around my neck, her fancy watch on my wrist; Mrs. Brown's face darkens. Her friends gather her close, circle the wagons until I depart. Out of the corner of my eye I see her grab the blue irises from their vase, hurl them across the room.

3. By the time I find out, Mr. Brown has been dead a year. I haven't seen him in a decade. I was not going to put out; he would not divorce Lucia. I never did ride in that blue Corvette. Soon I found myself a French photographer with a large dick and no wedding ring. I don't know if Mr. Brown ever found anyone. His obituary read, "Stand up guy, great husband, dad. Married sixty-six years. Pillar of the community. Charitable. A churchgoer." He once swore to me I was his church.

I have the offerings to prove it.

# The Narcissist's Confession

Before I was your wife
I was a narcissist.
Before that I was a dyke.

Before you I loved an artist. Big
cock. No ambition. I wanted him
to change. His cock shrank.

I poured sugar in his gas tank
to teach him a lesson.

What civilized person
acts like that?

Before I was your wife I loved
a woman. After sex
her scent lingered
on my upper lip.
Eau de Desperation.

But you, baby
smell like success, old,
east-coast money,
Episcopalian bebop, those
blue eyes focused Godward when
you come.

It took me forever,
stepping on them to get
to you. Sometimes
I wonder how
I managed to climb
over all those
bodies.

*"Cauchemar, Redondo Beach"* 2017

# The Seven Stages of Love—An L.A. Haiku-Noir Sequence

**the lure**
bring your tender love
to the city, 8th floor, the
door's ajar. find me!

**the operating instructions**
she explicitly
told me how to please her, but
then, she always lied.

**the truth**
as she walked away
she said, yes, I love women.
I just don't love you.

**the rationalization**
life's cruel casting call:
I can play taller, blonder,
but I can't play you.

**the big missing**
if matter cannot
be created or destroyed,
is she still out there?

**the acceptance**
so tired tonight. you'd
think the bottom had dropped out
of my intentions.

**the bullet dodged**
deep in my breathing
I stand outside of myself
and see me, breathing.

## Portrait of a Woman's Vagina as an Aerial Photograph

Look, he says, you can see the tillage, how it's broken into parcels, gerrymandered into neat little exploitations. The long-legged stretch of yellow hills, the sweet divide and that grassy mound, don't you see it? It's a construct: a torso complete with wetlands, vulva, and thighs. She's quite a spread, her legs straight as a virgin's, ankles straining like restless nuns. When she ran, she rivered, stars strewed before her, an embrace. She ran south, toward her savior, the only one who could moisten her, wet her down to bedrock, fill her with all that diverted water, the icy quench that pooled in her hollows. Look, he says, don't you see the blue? How it lapped her up, swallowed and made her a fertile field? Just added water.

# After My Lover Cheats on Me for the Third Time

she feeds me caviar, and peaches out of season, washes dishes in the nude, body flush against the sink, breasts sloping, teasing the suds. I can't help myself, sidle up behind, her flawless ass tight against my belly. Reach into the sudsy water, smear white froth on her nipples, feel them contract in my fists. To placate me she dons the turban I brought from Istanbul, stares into the beveled mirror of her vanity, a sliver of distortion widening her gaze. She's rouged her nipples. Darkened her lips. Kohled her amygdaloid eyes. *I have a vagina like a hastily packed suitcase,* she warned the first time I went down on her, but I liked it. I thought she was modest. Well-bred. Now I know how much she likes to travel. *It's funny,* she says. *I wouldn't cheat if you wouldn't judge.* Tonight when I let her make love to me, I try not to dwell on her serial betrayals, my focus above her head, out the window. Caressing the sky: a conga line of palm trees, slim-hipped lovelies, like teenaged girls—their awkward sway. *I like the sound the Santa Anas make, rustling the fronds,* I say. A shimmy. A tambourine. *Rats live in the palms,* my lover cautions. She frightens me so I'll cling more tightly. So when she lets go, there's recoil. Outside, our neighbor blasts vintage *Los Lobos* from his car. The tall palms gossip with the wind. After she comes, my lover falls asleep too easily. I can hear scavengers, sparring in the dark. Raccoons, maybe, or coyotes. It almost sounds like they're laughing. I want in on the joke.


*("I have a vagina like a hastily packed suitcase." Nikki Glaser, 2019 Netflix Special)*

# When

The regret that hides out inside our eyes when we say goodbye
when we see each other one last time when we wish we'd never
laid eyes on each other when we know for certain we've fallen
out of love when we realize we've made a mistake
when he back-pedals apologies and I grab his hand out of habit

and there's that fucking spark

and then there's him, pulling me in
when I'm fragile and he has the upper hand
when he sticks his tongue down my throat
when I get that swirly feeling in my cunt

when I want him to stop when I don't want him to stop
when he slips his hand inside my jeans when he wedges
his thumb inside my panties when I ache for the thrust of him

when he pushes me onto the bed when he takes my breasts in his hands
when his tongue moves down my body when I admit
he knows best how I like it when he admits he can't live without me

The regret that hides out inside my body
when my husband gets back in town.

# Driven—A Southern California Love Poem

Your cock is a traffic jam on the 405, nosing its way in, bumper to bumper with my on-ramp, those steel balls jostling. Your cock is better than a GPS. It always knows where to go. Who knew you were such a big rig operator, blue eyes mapping my terrain, right hand on the gear shift between my thighs, your stop and go mantra as you negotiate my freeway, accelerating into my turns. That expert downshift, firm grip of your hands on my steering wheel, guiding me up the next hilly grade, merging into the fast lane, signaling your intention. You drive me to distraction, to Nirvana, to Van Nuys. Take me to the Top of Topanga, those exhilarating switchbacks, the blinding glory of oncoming headlights. Oh Baby, don't ever take your eyes off this road.

## College Roommates

I asked for it, coming
home 2am, disheveled,
reeking sex. Every
weekend for a year.

It was my fault,
always in his face,
those skimpy clothes,
teasing him
with my inaccessibility.
I knew he knew
I was giving it away.

I wasn't surprised when
he sat in wait, pushed me
up against the dresser,
grabbed my breasts,
tore at my blouse,
ripped my skirt, shoved
himself into me, even
then, only half-hard.

I didn't mind the rape.
It was the softness I minded,
how he couldn't get it up
when it mattered.
I fell for hard men
with bad intentions.
Not men who loved me.

We never spoke of it
but his shame hung in the air,
that hangdog apology
in his eyes,
the unrequited love
that spoiled him for
anyone else.

*(for D.K.)*

*"Warhol, DTLA" 2015*

## Subterranean Lovesick Clues

1.
I remember listening
to Bob Dylan in Donna Melville's attic bedroom, 3 a.m.
We were drinking her daddy's bourbon, playing
*Subterranean Lovesick Blues* over and over,
memorizing it word by mumbled word.

*Johnny's in the basement,*
*mixing up the medicine, I'm on the pavement,*
*thinkin' 'bout the government...* Donna passed me the bottle.

The bourbon made me sick but I took a swig anyway.
I didn't want her to think I was a lightweight.
The word might get around.

*Maggie comes fleet foot, face full of black soot...*

Donna took the bottle to her lips, her moon face flushed,
beautiful. She was my first Catholic and I was in awe
of the certainty of her faith, couldn't take my eyes off
the lucky gold crucifix that dangled between her breasts.

"What do you think *Freewheelin'* means?"
We were on the bed, pretending to study
the album cover, Dylan and some blond
on a New York street, looking happy. "I think it means
fuck the consequences, just do what you want," I said.

Drunk, reckless, soon I'm ready to do what I want—
let my hand slip from the album jacket to Donna's left breast.
Her sharp intake of breath. My tom-tom heart.

*Look out kid, it's somethin' you did God knows when but you're doin' it again...*

These were the moments I lived for at 13: the hot, disheveled solace
of Donna's attic room, her clueless family asleep below,
Dylan's growl on the stereo,
Donna in my arms, her lips on mine, her tongue down my throat,
Fingers fumbling with my zipper.

2.
*Get dressed get blessed try to be a success...*

3.
Donna hits the Confessional.
"Father, forgive me for I have sinned."

*I* am that sin. I listen in.

"I kissed a girl," says my girl.
"You'll go to hell," says the desiccated
man in the box.

*4.*
*light yourself a candle...*
*you can't afford the scandals...*

5.
The Gospel According To St. Donna:

She is the innocent,
I am the sin.
I am the bad girl
That let the sin in.

6.
I remember listening
to Bob Dylan in Donna Melville's
attic bedroom, 3 a.m., the last time
I drank her daddy's bourbon,
the last time we ever touched.

This was the moment I dreaded at 14:
Afraid of the spark, afraid of her own ignition—
Donna changed the rules.

Jesus had entered the bedroom.

*"Lost Girl, 6th & Spring, DTLA"* 2015

"See ya," Donna said as she walked me
out of her life.
"Soon?" I asked. (A girl can dream, right?)
"Sure," she said.

7.
She didn't call.
I didn't call back.

*You don't need a weather man to know which way the wind blows...*

## Out of Body

She puts bowls on the table,
fixates on the scarred oak union,
digs her resentment into the grooves.

This is how he knows her:

She yawls.
Drowns him
out.

He eats her temporal lobe. Skim milk splashes
in the bowl. 5% body fat;
a new low.

Riddle: When is a promise like a bayonet?

I've been meaning to tell you.
A woman betrayed in a breakfast nook
does not constitute a poem.

Her dead mother reaches through the wall,
throws the marriage in her face.

Her husband grabs his bowl and a spoon.

*Sit down, darling,* he says.
*Open wide.*

# LARCENY: A Story in Eleven Parts

**In which 18-year-olds Victoria and Debi flee Los Angeles in Debi's blue Toyota Camry, and take the Pacific Coast Highway North with only a smattering of stars to light their way...**

### Into the Dark
The night highway crawls with creatures. Moths headfirst into the windshield, lizards, mice, besotted by headlights, crush flat beneath their tires. Sheltered. Stupid, the girls pick up a stranger. Thinking this is his lucky day, longhaired Danny tumbles into the back seat.

### Back Story
When Victoria moved in with Debi's family, junior year, her mom never realized she was missing. Now Victoria surveys her flawless skin, full lips, and thick blond hair in the rearview mirror; sees instead her mother's eyes, her dead daddy's smile.

### Just Outside of Pismo Beach: An Adventure!
Their route mirrors the shoreline. They speed to outdistance the past. Victoria tallies roadkill. It makes her think of her dad. When she tosses their purses in the back seat with Danny, he recalls the first time he snapped a cat's neck, but stops short of telling.

### Luck of the Draw
Debi's fingers run through her kinky black curls. She's ironed her hair into submission, endured the dryer, hair rolled large in rinsed, frozen orange juice cans. Jagger struts out of the radio. Debi hums off-key.

### Choices
If he has a choice, Danny'd go for the brunette. The blonde is hotter, but she looks like trouble. Somehow, trouble always finds him. *Where you headed?* Victoria asks. Danny looks from one girl to the other. *Hell in a handbasket,* he grins.

**The Low Down**
Debi wants Victoria's beauty. Victoria wants Debi's mom. Each dances in the other's castoff, each glows in the dark. Danny susses their singular affection. He's a good observer, an only child. Danny wants only their wallets.

**Night Swim**
The Lorelei moon lures the trio off-course. Tempted, they exit the highway, strip down to their skivvies, hurl themselves into the sea. Danny revels in the half-naked beauties, cavorting just for him in the moonlight. Out of their depth, Debi's fingers accidentally brush Victoria's left breast. As they come together, breathless, past the breakers, the peace is almost unbearable.

**Truth or Dare**
Midnight confessions. Danny never finished high school. Victoria's afraid of men. Debi takes the dare. Climbs the retaining wall and howls like a lunatic. Better this than her secrets spilled. When the big wave washes over her, Debi stands her ground. When Danny grabs her, anyway, she licks his face.

**On the Road Again**
Debi tends to dwell. Night driving clears her head. She chews a strand of her hair, sips vodka out of an Evian bottle. She misses Freddy's thick cock. Wonders why she ever left him. Approaching Morgan Hill, Debi finds a motel, reckons Danny owes her and Victoria for the ride.

**Karma: The Condensed Version**
It's the best day of Danny's life. In slumber, *he looks like baby Jesus,* Victoria sighs. Debi rescues their wallets from Danny's backpack. His, too. The North Star beckons. They'll make San Francisco by morning. The motel air conditioner's rattle masks their departure.

## The Last Leg

Victoria drives while Debi counts Danny's money. The Toyota eats up the highway, a rocket to their nascent future. She'll buy souvenirs in the city, maybe a gift for her mom. When Debi sticks her head out the window, even Victoria's chatter can't drown out the sound the wind makes.

*"Loft View, 8th Floor, DTLA"* 2017

## Acknowledgments

I'm grateful to Cynthia Atkins, Francesca Bell, Michelle Bitting, Chanel Brenner, Frank X. Gaspar, Tony Gloeggler, Jack Grapes, Richard Jones, Ellaraine Lockie, Clare MacQueen, Tony Magistrale, Tresha Haefner-Rubinstein, and Kelly Grace Thomas Vojdani, for their ongoing love, brilliance, and support. Thanks to my publisher, Raymond Hammond, for his generosity and wisdom. And thank you to my beloved Fancher, who knows me so well and loves me still.

## Previous Publications in Order of Appearance

## Photographs

CPSIA information can be obtained
at www.ICGtesting.com
Printed in the USA
FSHW011020270321
79850FS